HALLOWEEN

Artful
HALLOWEEN

31 Frightfully Elegant Projects

by SUSAN WASINGER

LARK CRAFTS
Asheville

Editor: LINDA KOPP
Art Director: SUSAN WASINGER
Photographer: SUSAN WASINGER
Cover Designer: KRISTI PFEFFER

LARK CRAFTS

An Imprint of Sterling Publishing
387 Park Avenue South
New York, NY 10016

If you have questions or comments about
this book, please visit: larkcrafts.com

Library of Congress Cataloging-in-Publication Data

Wasinger, Susan.
  Artful Halloween : 31 frightfully elegant projects / Susan Wasinger. -- 1st ed.
      p. cm.
  Includes index.
  ISBN 978-1-4547-0247-4 (pbk. : alk. paper)
  1. Halloween decorations. 2. Handicraft. I. Title.
  TT900.H32W37 2012
  745.594'1646--dc23

                              2011042357

10 9 8 7 6 5 4 3 2 1

First Edition

Published by Lark Books, A Division of
Sterling Publishing Co., Inc.
387 Park Avenue South, New York, NY 10016

Text © 2012, Susan Wasinger
Photography © 2012, Susan Wasinger

Distributed in Canada by Sterling Publishing,
c/o Canadian Manda Group, 165 Dufferin Street
Toronto, Ontario, Canada M6K 3H6

Distributed in the United Kingdom by GMC Distribution Services,
Castle Place, 166 High Street, Lewes, East Sussex, England BN7 1XU

Distributed in Australia by Capricorn Link (Australia) Pty Ltd.,
P.O. Box 704, Windsor, NSW 2756 Australia

ISBN 13: 978-1-4547-0247-4

For information about custom editions, special sales, and premium and corporate purchases, please contact
Sterling Special Sales Department at 800-805-5489 or specialsales@sterlingpub.com.

Requests for information about desk and examination copies available to college and university professors must
be submitted to academic@larkbooks.com. Our complete policy can be found at www.larkcrafts.com.

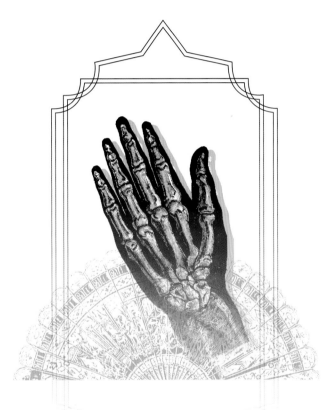

This book is dedicated to all of you—all of us—who know and love the power of

hands. Who like to use them on things other than keyboards and remote controls.

Who like to make things and reach out with them for all that is

good, and sound, and handmade...

Artful HALLOWEEN

PROJECTS

A Happier Halloween

Okay, full disclosure: Halloween hasn't always been my favorite holiday. In fact, in the past few years, Halloween has become downright scary to me. And I don't mean because of the ghosts and witches and zombies milling about. It had become so frightfully commercialized, overwrought with cringe-worthy plastic decorations, tart-y getups, and high-fructose junk foods. Halloween had begun to lose me, and I suspect was becoming uncomfortably tawdry for many of us. Americans will spend billions (yes, with a "b") on Halloween this year alone, and both the pragmatic and the creative sides of me think we deserve a whole lot more aesthetic whiz bang for all those big bucks.

It was time to dig into the deep, dark, and impishly twisted roots of Halloween to find new inspiration for a more elegant and stylish take on the season. I wanted to decorate for Halloween with stuff I make with my own two hands. But those things need to be beautiful, to add to the ambience of my home instead of shattering it. Luckily, grim but fetching muses were close at hand: It was time to summon the spirits of Steam Punk, to imagine visits to an alchemist's lab, or a medieval workshop. It was necessary to invoke all the gloriously ghoulish symbolism of this time of year including: owls, bats, snakes, spiders, full moons, groping hands, and staring eyes, each of these oozing a devilish charm and graphic intensity. Lastly, there were the pumpkins themselves to consider. No self-respecting Halloween could be complete without them. But it would never suffice to just carve up another pumpkin. Something new and different had to be done. On this crop of pumpkins, ornamental flourish runs rampant—some figured like a matador's cape, others studded and spiked like a medieval mace. Some, however, are willing to just dress up pretty for the night. In the end, who says a splattering of "blood" or a smattering of monsters or the patterings of a spider's many feet can't make for a more welcoming home? Read on to see if these pages aren't haunted with a brand new Halloween spirit.

TRADITIONS
Halloween Runs Deep

Our modern-day Halloween has its roots deep in the collective soul: It borrows from rich Celtic tradition, mixing in Catholic and Roman religious rites and beliefs, and finishing it all off with a smattering of rituals from the Harvest festivals of European folk cultures. It's a heady mix of the divine and the disturbing.

Halloween is a holiday of transition: It falls in autumn as summer gives way to winter, as the days go from light to dark, and the world from green and growing to barren and dead. It is the moment when the great harvest has past and a long, cold, hungry winter looms ahead. It is uncertain and foreboding. It is also a night of another powerful transition, "All Hallows Eve." Celebrated the day before All Saints Day, it is traditionally the one night in the year when the dead can return to walk the earth. This is the obvious genesis of all the modern Halloween trappings to do with ghosts, zombies, and skeletons. This terrifying notion prompted the Celts to light bonfires and wear costumes to ward off these roaming ghosts. Thus our obsession with costuming ourselves like these wandering ghouls, but also like superheroes who might be able to banish them.

The tradition of "trick-or-treating" probably dates back to early Soul Day's Parades in Britain where poor citizens would beg for "Soul Cakes" in return for a promise to pray for the benefactor's dead relatives.

The carving of pumpkins is rumored to also have started in the British Isles, where in earlier times, a beet or a turnip was hollowed out and lit with a candle from within and then left on the doorstep to ward off evil spirits. Practical revelers in the New World decided to use a pumpkin since it is larger, more abundant, and much easier to carve.

THE ANNUAL
Pumpkin Party

A neighborhood tradition endures...

**For the thirteenth
year running, the annual
Pumpkin Party
closes off an entire
neighborhood block**

to celebrate Halloween with family
and friends amid live music, tables
laden with food, and pumpkins,
lots and lots of pumpkins. The
festivities start in late afternoon
when tables are set with pumpkin-
carving tools for the arrival of the
trailer-load of orange orbs from
a farm east of town. The creative
carving begins in earnest, with
artists of all ages taking a stab at
it. As dusk falls, the pumpkins find
their place on stepped platforms
that are rigged to the house for
the purpose of maximum display.
The pumpkins are wired for light,
and then as everyone gathers in
the darkness, the guest of honor
flips the switch to illuminate
countless pumpkin-y grins and
grimaces. While the music plays
on, partygoers parade past the
pumpkins, pointing out the ones
they carved or choosing a par-
ticular favorite. For a holiday that
is traditionally grim and spooky,
steeped in the dark arts, this cel-
ebration is unusually full of light
and friendship and frolicsome fun.

TOOLS

What You Need

Most of what you need you already have. Any crafter worth their salt has amassed a tool

or two by now, and the projects in this book don't stray too far from the usual suspects

in your tool chest or junk drawer. Most of the tools listed are so common that

they need no commentary. Still, a list and a caveat or two follow:

The Standard List
of **TOOLS**
a partial list

Scissors
for both paper and fabric

Paintbrushes
in a variety of sizes

A small tool kit
with hammer and screwdriver

Measuring devices
ruler, yardstick, tape measure

A wide variety of pens
regular writing pens, fat markers, metallic pens

Needle-nosed pliers

Hole punch

Stapler

Drills, ovens, sewing machines, and other power tools: There are projects (like the aprons, the tin man, and cupcake toppers) that require a power tool to complete. The oven is pretty straightforward, either you can turn one on or you can't, but the sewing machine and the drill require a little practice. Consider asking a friend to help. Or, if you decide to go it alone, practice repeatedly first on a scrap.

Computer, printer, scanner, copy machine: The modern world requires a bit of technical savvy. Even crafting leans on a pixel here and there. Some of the templates at the back of the book need to be enlarged and copied. A copier does this with ease, as does the scanner/computer/printer triad.

Craft blade and cutting mat: The best tools in the world to cut intricate shapes out of paper, cardboard, and even felt. A self-healing mat is the perfect partner to the blade. Take your time when using cutting tools like this to avoid any painful and unwanted slices.

Rubber stamps: Used to great effect in the note card project, rubber stamps pack a lot of fun into a small footprint. Craft stores and online sources have a seemingly infinite variety. Be sure to choose an ink pad that is larger than your rubber stamp.

Newspaper and paper plates: You'll need some disposable items to handle the inevitable messes. Use newspaper to cover surfaces (so you don't find that your table, after a painting project, suddenly starts glowing in the dark). Small paper plates and plastic utensils are great for mixing paint. A face mask is smart when using spray paints.

MATERIALS

What You'll Use

Each project in this book contains a detailed list of the materials needed. But I just want to reassure you right up front, I kept it very simple. There was no going to the ends of the earth to source anything. Most all of the parts and pieces can be found at your local craft store or the occasional hardware emporium.

CRAFT STORES are wonderful places, full to the rafters of materials and tools for the making of things. Most of the materials used in this book were found at craft stores, including brightly colored poster paper, embroidery floss, acrylic craft paints, spray paints in a wide variety of shades and types, and metallic paints that can be brushed on, squeezed into place, or stroked on with a pen. All sorts of stickers for the decorating of pumpkins were found, as well as laser-cut paper and stencils. There is a nice selection of tacks, pins, and small nails. Craft stores are also an excellent source for the small hardware, beads, and baubles—much of it from the jewelry-making section—for use in the embellishment of pumpkins. Basic supplies like wire, string, twine, and pipe cleaners abound. The craft store is also the go-to source for glues, tapes, adhesives, and finishes. Even the more obscure materials can be found here, like shrink plastic, magnets, crepe paper, and glass gems.

FABRIC STORES are a great source for felt, fabric, lace, ribbon, heavyweight thread, and embroidery floss.

HARDWARE STORES are where to go for lots of useful crafting supplies. You can find nuts, bolts, wing nuts, the fence posts needed for the ghoulish yard art, wire in all gauges, and materials, twine, and string, too. Look here for florist's tape and stem wire. Specialty nail heads are also to be had, along with metal buckets in all shapes and sizes.

THE INTERNET is a fabulous source for unusual items. Rather than driving all over town to find intriguing materials, these days they're just a Google search or two away. I found many of the gorgeous nailheads and upholstery tacks online that I used to decorate pumpkins. For even more possibilities, try searching online auction sites.

JUNK STORES, GARAGE SALES, RECYCLE BINS – A few projects use odd tidbits as a jumping–off point, like the place cards that use vintage photos, or the disembodied hands that require vintage ladies' gloves. Part of the fun of this kind of shopping is that you never know exactly what you will find, ensuring that your finished project will be one-of-a-kind.

TECHNIQUES
How It's Done

Some of the best crafters are shameless dilettantes, fearless, optimistic attempters of any and all things no matter how cockamamie they might sound (which is what I love about crafters). Most of the projects in this book require more attitude than expertise. Nothing is too hard or beset with too steep a learning curve. The most important technique, employed over and over again in this book, is the simple willingness to give it a try.

If you can hold a paintbrush, shake a paint can, hammer a tack, use a pair of scissors, then you're already in possession of 90 percent of the skill needed to complete 80 percent of the projects in this book. Many of the techniques–like simple hand stitching or painting polka dots or using a rubber stamp–are things you learned so long ago, you might assume you were born knowing them.

A couple of projects require a modicum of skill. The aprons, for instance, will need a sewing machine and the attendant ability to power up, thread, and drive one. However, if you can sew a straight line and turn a corner, you are enough of an expert seamster to carry on.

Other projects, like the Halloween printed cards, require some hand skills in using a craft blade to cut out a traced shape. This mandates more a level of focus and degree of patience than it does a quotient of skill.

Can you bend wire? Draw a straight line? Thread a needle? Maybe you can. But the real question is, can you follow directions? Can you look at a picture and say, "Hey, I can do that, too!" Because each of the projects in this book contains extensive written and illustrated instructions. These how-tos give you plenty to go on, whether you are a visual or a literal learner. The projects were chosen on the basis of their accessibility to the average crafter. If you can put one foot in front of the other and count to 10, you are well on your way to making everything in this book.

And of course, when all else fails, then blaze a trail and do it your own way! No one is forcing you to follow the directions, there is no one "right" way. If you are more of the "question authority" personality type, please think of the step-by-step instructions as mere inspirational guidelines.

The Alchemist's Book
PENNANT GARLAND

Old books have a venerability, gravity, and a whiff of menace all their own. This decorative garland takes a page out of an alchemist's book. Each vintage page is photocopied over with an image of bones, bugs, or bats, making them look like the workbook of a demented scientist. The images to copy, from skeletons to snakes, are not hard to find online. There are even more from specialty clip art publishers who sell them in books for scanning or photocopying or on CDs to print out on your computer. For the pennant "flags," find a small vintage hard-cover book at a garage sale or used bookseller. String them up to make a festive yet fearsome garland that is pretty but potent.

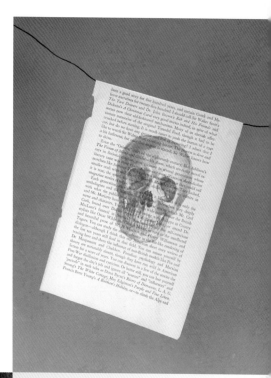

MATERIALS

vintage black-and-white illustrations of spooky things like bats, snakes, skulls, spiders, ravens, etc.

old hard-cover book, smallish (about 5 x 8 inches) works best

white glue, double-stick tape, or glue stick

string—black, white or natural color

TOOLS

scissors

a computer with printer or a photocopier

how to:

1 Tear pages out of the old hard-cover book. Locate and size the image you want to copy. Load the vintage pages into the paper feeding tray of your photocopier or printer. Print or copy the image onto the page (photo A).

2 Cut a length of string about 10 feet long (you can go longer or shorter depending on your needs). Fold down the top edge of the vintage page about $^1/_2$-inch. Fold it back and run a bead of glue, glue stick, and/or strip of tape along the inside of the edge. Leave a loose end of string about 1-foot long for hanging the garland. Run the string under the glued edge as shown, and press down to encase the string in the folded edge. Let dry (photos B and C).

3 Leave about $^1/_2$-inch of string between this page and the next page you add. Work all the way across the string, leaving another foot of free string on the other end for hanging. For a 10-foot string, you will need about 15 or 16 pages. The garland is easy to fold for storage. Just stack the pages back, and store like a book (photo D).

NOTE: You can choose to leave more open string between your pennant pages if you prefer the look, or if you have a lot of ground to cover. Both versions look frightfully cool.

MATERIALS

small vintage photos
from junk stores

cardstock in brown or rust

plain tags with string from
the office supply store
(these are about 3 x 1 1/2 inches)

optional: LED votive candle

TOOLS

pen

scissors

optional: pushpin

It's an odd fact that old photos of people you don't know, who lived a long time ago, are just creepy and strange. Not to be disrespectful or anything, but staring into the eyes of a person who is no longer among the living can just make the hair on the back of your neck stand up. It is reminiscent of a séance. So what better way to invite a rowdy cadre of departed spirits to your next dinner party than to use old photos for the place cards. An old shoebox, filled with unidentified photos found at a junk store, inspired the idea. A couple of snips of paper and a simple store-bought tag complete the spooky effect.

In Mexico at Halloween, they picnic on the graves of their departed loved ones...

23

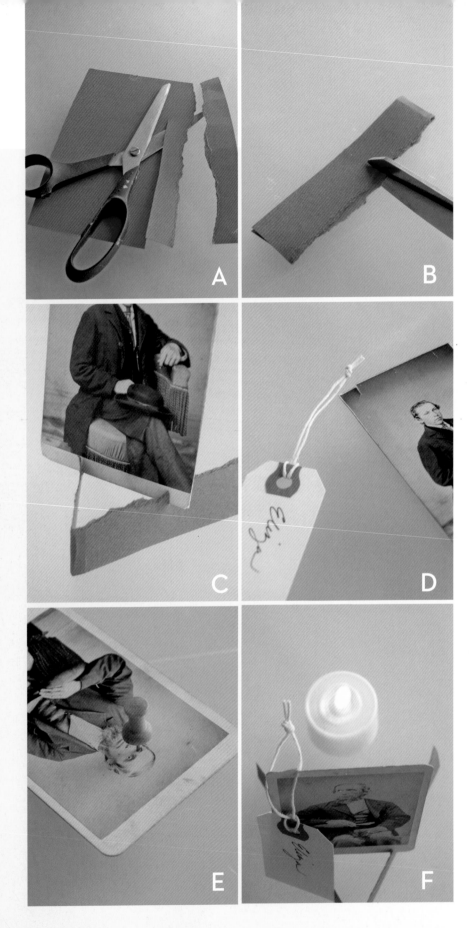

how to:

1 Tear a piece of cardstock 1 inch wide x about 8 inches long. The bottom edge of the paper strip should be cut; the top edge should be torn (photo A).

2 Fold the paper strip in half. Make a $1/4$-inch snip through both layers of the strip about 2 inches from the centerfold (photo B).

3 Set the paper base with the cut side down, fold to the front. Place the photo into the snipped slots as shown in the photo so it stands up (photo C).

4 Nip a tiny slit with the point of the scissors into the top left edge of the photo as shown. Write the name of your guest in your best old-timey cursive on a store-bought tag with string. Tie a knot toward the end of the two strings, slip one of the strings into the slit to hold in place. Make sure the name falls toward the front (photo D).

5 OPTIONAL EXTRA CREEPINESS: Okay, this will test just how creepy you feel like being. If you dare, take a pushpin and poke out the eyes of the subject in the photo (photo E). Make sure the holes go all the way through. Set up your little placeholder with a small LED-powered "candle" behind it. Once the lights dim down low, the eyes in the photo will glow red, giving these name holders an even eerier quality (photo F).

Or...

Add a second set of snipped slits toward the front of the base and lay the name tag in on its side as shown at right.

Charles

Dr. Augen
Fri. 13th 2:30pm

blood orange
artichoke hearts
leg of lamb
rib eye
deviled eggs
dog b

MAGNETS

Eyes are the windows to the soul; they also are the seat of consciousness, and that fact makes these disembodied eyes seem extremely sinister. This project recycles images from fashion magazines to make glass eyes that can be used as strange and watchful sentinels on your bulletin board or refrigerator. Even beautiful eyes can look menacing when they stare you down and never, ever blink first.

MATERIALS

recycled magazines with lots of ads and large portraits. (fashion mags work great)

wax paper to protect work surface

special glue that adheres to glass—must be transparent

large clear glass "gems" or "half-marbles" that are about $1^1/_2$ inches across

small disk magnets (about 1-inch diameter)

optional: pinbacks to turn these into brooches

TOOLS

scissors

pen

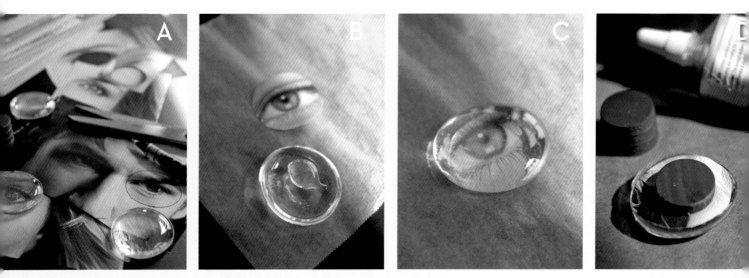

how to:

1 Look through the recycled magazines to find close-up pictures of faces where the eyes are prominent. Use your glass gem to "test" the image. Place the gem over the eye, and see how it looks. If you like the choice, use a pen to trace around the outside of the gem. With scissors, cut out the eye. Cut just to the inside of your line so that the image is just slightly smaller than the glass gem and there will be no overhang (photo A).

2 Put the eye cutout faceup on the wax paper. Squeeze a pea-sized bead of glass glue on the back (flat side) of your glass gem (photo B).

3 Press the glass gem onto the eye cutout, being careful to center the gem over the eye. Pressing hard pushes any air bubbles out the edges and makes the eye show clearly. Hold in place for a few seconds till the glue starts to set. Let dry (photo C).

4 Once the glue is dry and the glass gem isn't sliding around anymore, turn the glass gem eyeball over facedown. Use a smaller dollop of the glass glue on the back side of the glass gem (this will be where the magazine paper is). Glue a magnet into place on the center back of the glass eye (photo D).

Or...

Keep an eye on all your friends. Make these into giftable brooches to festoon a lapel or perch on the brim of a hat. Instead of gluing on a magnet, buy self-adhesive, metal pinbacks at a craft store and center them on the back of the "glass eye."

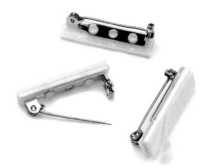

Button & Bead
SPIDERS

Creepy, crawly, scurrying, scuttling... invite these little eight-legged guests to your Halloween feast. Elegant and edgy spiders made from buttons and beads and copper wire add a note of whimsy and a little bit of menace to your table. These are easy and fun to make, in all sizes and shapes. Put them on a plate, hang them off the candlesticks, mix them in with the silverware, this might be one time your dinner companions won't mind finding a bug in their food.

MATERIALS

20-gauge copper wire

transparent tape

medium to large metal button
with shank

large round bead

TOOLS

needle-nose pliers

wire cutters

how to:

1 Choose a metal shank button for the body and a round bead that looks good with it for the spider's head. The shank of the button needs to be big enough to accommodate 8 pieces of wire, and the bead needs a hole big enough for the wire to fit through.

2 Cut 9 pieces of copper wire, each about 8 inches long. Set one piece aside and bundle the other eight together so that their ends line up. Wrap a piece of transparent tape about 1/2 inch long around the center of the bundle to keep all eight pieces together.

3 Slide the bundled wire through the button shank until the wire is centered (photo A).

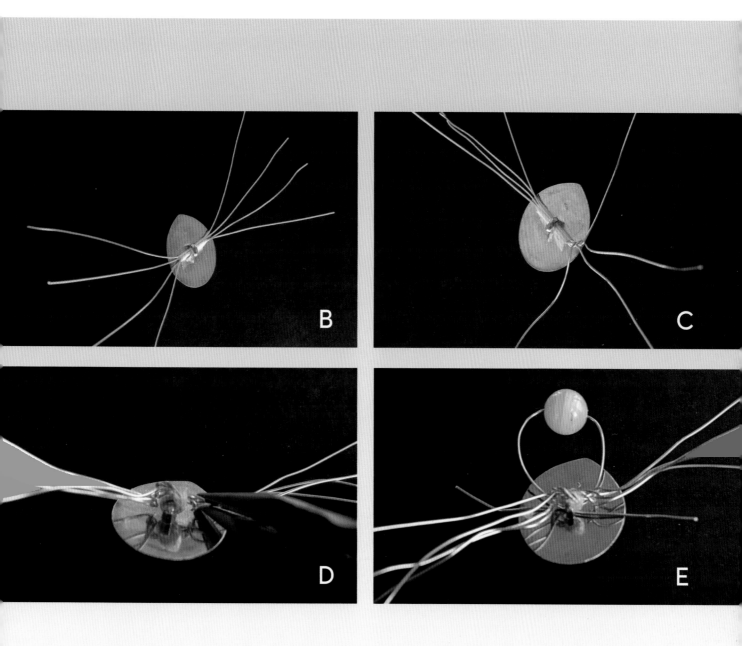

B

C

D

E

4 Tear off two pieces of scotch tape about ¼ inch wide. Use this skinny tape to strap the wire bundle down to the button on either side of the shank as shown. Spread the individual wires open. These will be the spider's legs (photo B).

5 Starting on one side of the shank, twist the wire on the far right together with the wire to its left. Twist again so the wire that was the farthest on the right still is, though now it has two twists around the adjacent wire (photo C).

6 Starting with the wire second from right, twist it around the wire immediately adjacent to it on the left. Twist again as before (photo D).

7 Twist the third wire from the right around the wire immediately adjacent on its left. Twist again as before. Now all four legs are secured together.

8 Turn the button around and repeat steps 5 through 7 on the wires on the other side of the shank. Remove the tape "straps" that you applied in step 4.

9 With your needle-nose pliers, grab one twisted bundle of wire right where it comes out of the shank and bend it up and over the shank to the other side. Now grab the twisted bundle of wire close to the shank on the other side, and bend it up and over the shank in the other direction. Try to get these as tight to the shank as possible. This will "tie" the wire into the shank and keep the wire bundle of legs from slipping out.

10 Thread the bead onto the ninth piece of wire, centering it on the wire. Gently bend the wire in half around the bead and hold it over the button shank. Thread one end of the wire through the shank from right to left. Then thread the other end through from left to right. This will be a little challenging as you need to feed it around the other wires using the shank, but there should still be plenty of room. Pull the two ends in opposite directions through the shank to draw the button closer in. Stop pulling when there is a loop with about 1-inch of wire left on either side of the button (photo E).

11 Using your needle-nose or just fingers, twist the loop with the bead on it a few times to make the spider's neck. The neck should stay underneath the spider's body and the bead/head should sit right on the edge of the button body. Twist the other ends of this ninth wire together a few times to anchor this to the shank. Cut the wire ends close to the twists with the wire cutter (photo F).

12 Turn the spider over and bend out the legs evenly. Snip the wires so all the legs are of equal length (photo G).

13 Bend the leg down in a soft curve about halfway up the leg, right where the spider's knee would be. Repeat on all legs (photo H).

14 Grasp the very end of the leg of the spider with the tip of your needle-nose pliers. Turn the wire up in a tight curlicue to make the spider's foot. Repeat on all 8 legs (photo I).

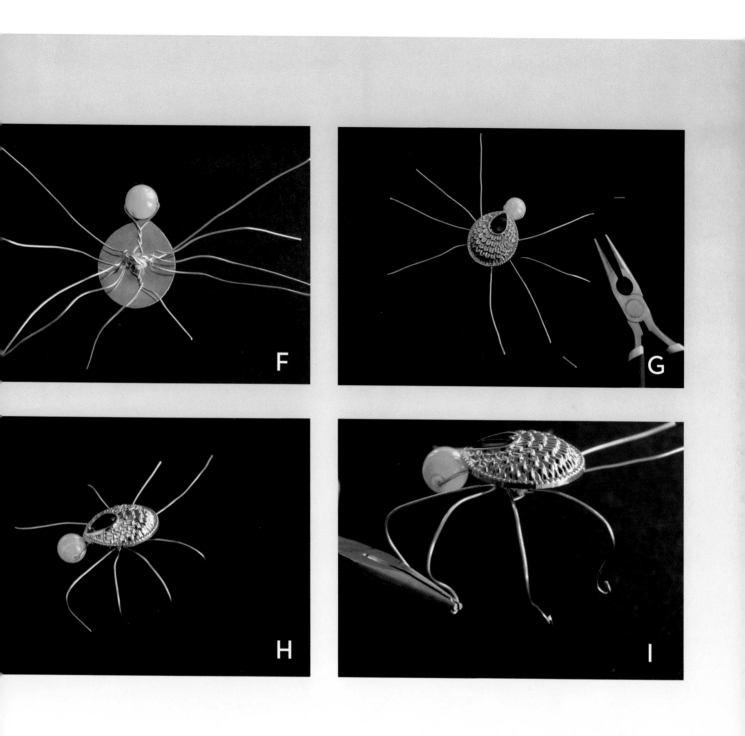

Disembodied
HAND-IN-GLOVE

The disembodied hand is a classic symbol of malice and mischief. This sinister installation, perfect for a mantel or console table or prominent shelf, evokes the evil lair of Hannibal Lecter or some other diabolical scientist. Vintage evening gloves and large glass jars or cloches are all that's needed to make the vignette work its dark magic. Bend the hands into a menacing, playful, or tortured gesture and they look like specimens from some dark experiment gone horribly wrong.

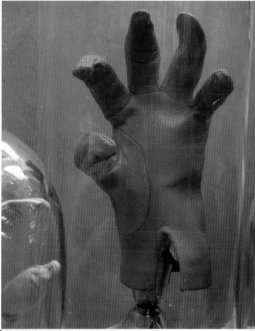

MATERIALS

vintage ladies' evening gloves in leather or cloth

large, wide-mouthed glass jars or glass cloches

pipe cleaners—five per glove
(at least 12 inches long)

cotton, wool, or polyester batting

miscellaneous stands
(see note for ideas)

TOOLS

wire cutters or craft scissors

 A

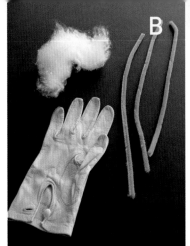 B

 C

 D

how to:

1 Start with some vintage evening gloves. Bins and boxes of these can often be found at junk stores. Hundreds of choices are also available at online auction sites as well. Black and red are nice, but those in light tan or peachy tones look especially creepy—like disembodied hands!

Glass jars, glass vases, and cloches give the installation its look of scientific veracity. Look for glass ware that is tall and wide enough for the glove and any stand you use. Glass vases can be left open on the top or lidded, or can be inverted to enclose the "hand" (photo A).

2 You'll need a pipe cleaner for every finger in the glove, as well as a small puff of batting (photo B).

3 Place the batting on the end of the pipe cleaner (photo C).

4 Fold the pipe cleaner and the batting down about 3½ inches so the batting is between two lengths of pipe cleaner (photo D).

5 Twist the two lengths of pipe cleaner together over and around the batting, to make a thick "finger." There should still be a few inches of pipe cleaner extending down below the finger. Repeat to make four more of these fingers. The "pinky" wants to be a little shorter and slimmer than the others, and the "thumb" shorter and thicker (photo E).

6 Carefully work one of the pipe cleaner and batting contraptions up into the finger of the glove. You have to kind of gently feed it into the glove and work it carefully so the batting stays wrapped around the pipe cleaner. Leave the long pipe cleaner end for now (photo F).

7 Work your way across the glove till all five fingers are stuffed. Gather the pipe cleaner ends together with a loose twist. You can fold these ends up into the body of the glove to give the hand some "bones." If these end pieces are too long and are showing below the bottom of the glove, cut them off with craft scissors or wire cutters. Add more stuffing in the palm of the hand, paying special attention to the area at the base of the thumb. Use your own hand as a guide as to where the batting should be thick and where there should be less. Tuck the stuffing up into the glove so none of it shows at the bottom. Now the hand is ready to be bent and molded into any shape or gesture you desire (photo G).

E

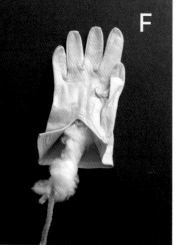

F

G

H

Note...

The hand can be simply propped up within your jar, vase, or cloche. Or if it is a flatter cloche style (like a cake cover), the hand can lie flat. If you have taller jars or cloches, and would prefer to stand your hand up higher, there are lots of ways to do that. Drill a hole in a small piece of wood (3 or 4 inches, square or round) and stand a rod or dowel (about 8 to 10 inches tall) in the hole. A little glue will keep the rod solid. Alternately, use candlesticks as stands. Even a plumbing part (flange) and a pencil make an adequate stand to keep your hands up (photo H).

Gone Batty
NOTE CARDS

I have a friend who avoids the Christmas Card, Seasonal Overload Disorder by sending out Halloween cards instead. They contain all the family news and well wishes for a wonderful year but come at a time when people actually have the time and energy to read it. These handmade note cards are a little bit spooky but with a nice dose of graphic chic. Easy to make with simple skills and tools, they're very flexible so no two cards need be alike.

MATERIALS

uncoated cardstock for note cards in soft colors like cream, gray, and light brown

cardstock for stencil

inked pad for stamping

craft paint in white and orange

envelopes

TOOLS

assorted rubber stamps

craft blade and cutting surface to cut bat stencil

straightedge/ruler

black felt tip or gel pen for outlining

masking tape

paintbrush

how to:

1 Fold the cardstock in half to make cards. Use the straightedge and craft knife to trim the folded cards down to a size that fits into your envelopes. Here the cards are trimmed to 5 x 7 inches to fit into a standard A7 envelope that is $7\frac{1}{4}$ x $5\frac{1}{4}$ inches.

2 Copy the bat template to size from page 124. Place it on the cardstock and cut around the outline to make the stencil. Keep both the stencil and the inner cut-away bat shape (photo A).

3 Place the stencil centered on the front of your note card and begin stamping over the opening with an inked stamp. Be sure to press firmly, but don't wiggle the stamp or your impression will be blurry. Before removing the stencil, trace around the inner edge of the bat stencil with the pen. Remove the stencil (photo B).

4 For the striped card, place the bat-shaped cutout from step 2 over the stamped area. Run masking tape—either vertically or horizontally—at intervals across the whole card (photo C). Paint over the entire surface. Don't overload the brush with paint; it gives the stripes a hand-painted look and really lets the brush strokes show (photo D). When dry, remove the tape and the bat, then do a second outline around the outside edge of the bat to finish (photo E).

Or... Some variations: Mask off the top two-thirds of the card, and brush a sweep of color along the bottom. Use a circle of cardstock to mask off a large moon shape behind the bat. Use the smaller bat stencil from page 124 to add some graphic appeal to the envelope.

Black Lace
VOTIVES

Black lace is the perfect combination of beauty and malice. It's the femme fatale of the trim aisle. If you are not quite ready to wear it, then by all means dress your table with it. These very simple-to-make votive holders borrow all the intricate handwork of the lace to make objects of exceptional filigreed loveliness in a project that takes just a few minutes to complete. Here are three different kinds of lace—including a double wrap of lacy beaded ribbon. The notions department at your local craft or sewing store should have lots of fun things to choose from.

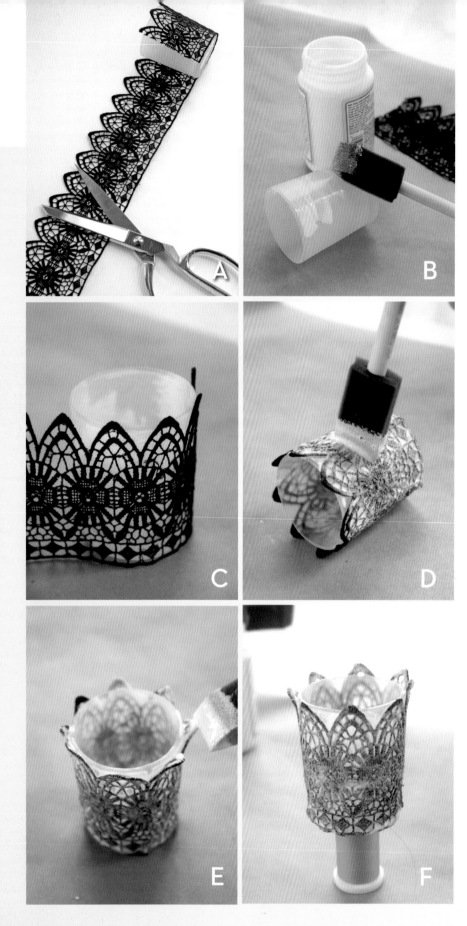

how to:

1 Wrap the votive holder in lace. Cut a piece long enough so the ends overlap just a little. Unwrap the holder (photo A).

2 Cover the surface of the votive holder with the decoupage glue. Let it sit a minute or two until the surface is tacky (photo B).

3 With the holder standing upright, wrap the lace all the way around it. Since the bottom of the votive holder is likely a bit smaller than the top, there will be a few pleats and bunches toward the base. Don't worry, the decoupage coating in the next step eliminates all ills (photo C).

4 Coat the entire surface of the votive holder with the decoupage medium. The foam brush is great for working the goo down into the nooks and crannies of the lace. Work firmly but gently, too, as too much wiggling might make the lace start to move around. Use the foam brush to press the lace down firmly on the glass (photo D).

5 The lacy peaks of this piece of trim extended up above the top edge of the votive glass. It was the perfect opportunity to give the glass a little extra dimension and shape by coaxing the edge to flair outward. The decoupage medium dries hard, so whatever shape you create will be retained once the medium dries completely (photo E).

6 Put the votives up on something to get them up off the ground so that the bottom edge doesn't stick to the tabletop. A spool of thread works great (photo F).

Blood-Spattered
PAPER BOUQUET

These delicate blooms carry a painful secret. A splatter of scarlet alludes to a violent past. A simple twist of paper, a spray of paint, and your imagination does the rest. Real flowers fade too fast, but this lovely crepe paper bouquet will long bear witness from its perch on mantel or hearth. If you want to take the effect to its logical conclusion, splash some drops of "blood" on the vase as well.

MATERIALS

crepe paper in cream and black

green floral wire stem

green floral tape

craft paint in a dark red

TOOLS

small paintbrush

scissors

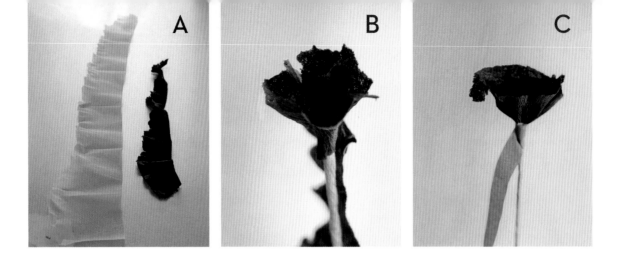

A   B   C

how to:

1 Tear a piece of black crepe paper about 12 to 15 inches long. Tear it on the diagonal so that it starts at a point and ends about 1½ to 2 inches wide (photo A). Tear a cream-colored piece of crepe paper that is about 24 to 28 inches long. It should start about 1½ to 2 inches wide and then end about 4 to 5 inches wide. You want the top edge of the strips be ruffled, so grab the crepe paper along the top edge and stretch it gently. This will make the top edge longer than the rest of the strip and creates rumpled, frothy, ruffled edges on your finished flowers.

2 To begin forming the flower, wrap the narrow end of the black crepe paper strip around one end of the green stem wire. Be sure to let the paper overhang the end a little to hide the end of the stem wire. Wrap the paper strip around and around, squeezing and twisting at the base of the paper and flaring out the top of the paper as you go. You will need to fold little pleats in the bottom of the paper as you wrap. Just keep thinking "tighter at the base, looser at the top" (photo B).

3 Once you have wrapped all the black paper onto the wire, give the base a final tight twist. Then secure the base of the paper with green florist tape. Be sure to stretch the tape slightly as you wrap. This allows it to really "grab" the paper and stem. Circle around the flower base several times, spiraling the green tape downward on the stem as you go (photo C).

4 Repeat the process, now with the cream-colored paper, again starting with the narrow end of the strip. Pay even more attention to pleating the base in this step. This really highlights the ruffle-y edge and ensures that the finished bloom is big and fluffy and falls open like a flower should (photo D).

5 Again, twist the base firmly, and begin wrapping the base tightly with florist's tape. This time work the green tape all the way down the length of the stem, and finish. You can finish with a piece of scotch tape to secure (photo E).

6 Thin the craft paint with a little water so it flows and spatters more easily. To "spray" the flowers with the faux blood, load up the paintbrush with paint, then run your (gloved) thumb over the brush to spatter the surface with paint droplets. Add as few or as many as you'd like (depending on how macabre you want the scene to appear). Alternatively, if this approach sounds too messy, tear off a strip of crepe paper, dip it in the paint, and drag it across the surface of the flower to add drips and drops (photo F).

D   E   F

Consider...

extending the mayhem to the vase, too. This vessel had an earlier life as an indifferent off-white junk store thing. A quick coat of glossy spray paint really brought out its detail. Take it further with some "blood" spatters using the same technique described for the flowers.

Spooky Spirits

BOTTLE WRAPS

Halloween is a season of spirits: some sinister, some festive. Here's a fun and simple way to wrap a bottled gift that conjures up the ghosts and ghouls and other dangerous creatures that haunt these darkest of nights. Nevermind that these spirits didn't get an official invitation, there's not a ghost of a chance that they'll be unwelcome.

MATERIALS

cardstock in black, white, and gold

crepe paper in black and cream

floral stem wire

glue dots or transparent tape

TOOLS

craft knife and cutting surface

glass, lid, etc. for tracing circle

pen

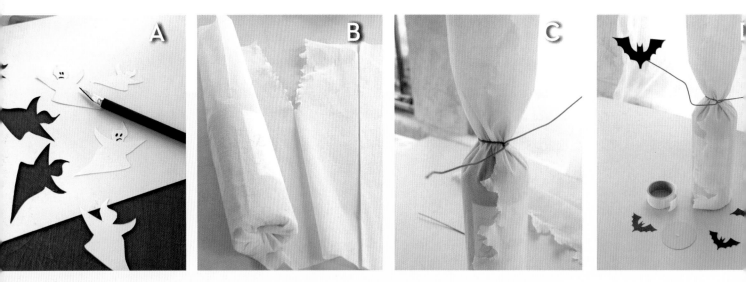

A B C

how to:

1 Print out the bat and ghost templates on page 124, and use them to cut the shapes out of the cardstock—ghosts out of the white cardstock, bats from the black. Using a small glass or lid, trace and cut out a circle about 2 to 3 inches across from the gold cardstock to make the moon (photo A).

2 Wrap the bottle in the crepe paper, leaving about 4 to 6 inches of extra paper at the top of the bottle and 3 or 4 inches at the bottom. The crepe paper should wrap around the bottle once or twice with several inches of overlap. Tear a jagged edge in the wrap. Once torn, pull and stretch the edge of the crepe paper to make it even more jagged and ruffled. Center this jagged edge on the front of the bottle. Fold up the excess at the bottom and secure with scotch tape (photo B).

3 Secure the crepe paper on the bottle using the stem wire as you would a twist tie wrapped around the bottle's neck. A couple wraps and a couple twists should do the trick (photo C).

4 Use the glue dots or a small piece of tape to attach the ghosts and/or bats to the wire. The moon should attach behind one of the larger bats. Bend the wires up and down at interesting angles to show off the figures to their best advantage (photo D).

5 Tear the top edge of the crepe paper around the bottle. Make it a jagged tear that angles up from the wire tie and spirals up through the various layers of crepe paper that wrap the bottle. Remember to stretch the edge of the paper for an extra ragged edge. The finished product looks like clouds (the white bottle) or smoke (the dark one).

Monstrously Adorable
CUPCAKE TOPPERS

Do you have a drawerful of kids' drawings of monsters? Or maybe a houseful of antsy kids who need to sit down and draw out their inner demons? This is the perfect fun project for either of those. These little mini cupcake toppers transfer the ephemeral to the tangible, using a lot of imagination and a little shrink plastic to make all those monsters just as real as can be.

You can either draw new monsters on the direct-draw variety of shrink plastic, or scan vintage monsters into your computer and print them out on the printable shrink plastic.

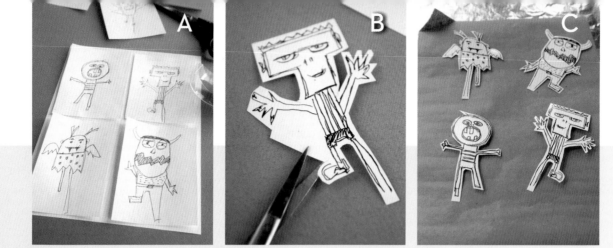

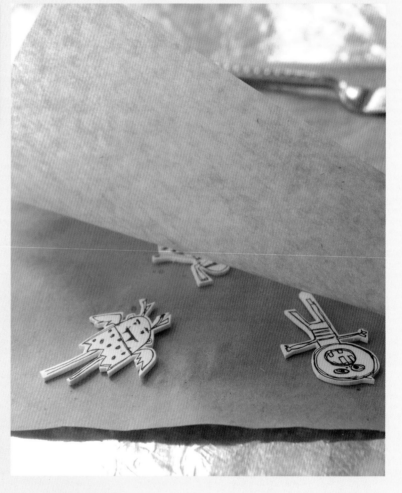

Tips

I had a lot of trouble with my shrink plastic rolling up and sticking to itself making these truly frightening blobs. I used the layer of paper bag under the shrink plastic for baking that the manufacturer suggested, but I added a layer of baking parchment on top of the little monsters for their stint in the oven. I weighted down the parchment with a fork on either end of the parchment just to make sure nothing could curl up. It worked like a charm every time! I also found that a regular-sized oven worked better for baking than a toaster oven. Just one girl's opinion.

how to:

1 If you have existing monster drawings, scan them into your printer and size them so they fit 4 up on an 8$\frac{1}{2}$ x 11 sheet. Follow manufacturer's instructions to print the monster drawings on the shrink plastic page. If you are drawing new monsters, cut the sheets of shrink plastic paper into four segments and draw a monster on each. The plastic shrinks to about $\frac{1}{3}$ its original size, so these monsters will be the perfect size for mini cupcakes. Bigger cupcakes might want monsters drawn on $\frac{1}{2}$ sheets of paper. Try to extend one leg of your monsters so they can stick into the cupcakes and be stable (photo A).

2 Use the sharp scissors to cut carefully around the monster drawings. Little snips work best, as the shrink plastic material can be slightly brittle (photo B).

3 Follow the manufacturer's instructions for baking and shrinking the plastic. Please read the notes at left to see what I found that works the best (photo C).

4 Once baked and cooled, spray the plastic monsters with non-toxic clear finish to keep the drawings from smearing. The monster toppers should be wiped clean with a damp cloth after use (photo at right).

Black Skeleton Flower GARLAND

Here is the perfect modern gothic embellishment for your mantel at Halloween. Cardstock, a gold pen, and some brassy brads come together to create a dark creation that is part flower, part skeleton, but still inexplicably elegant.

MATERIALS

black cardstock

gold or silver metallic pens

decorative brads like these square, brassy ones

permanent tape

black cord, string, or yarn

TOOLS

craft knife and cutting surface

scissors

small-hole punch

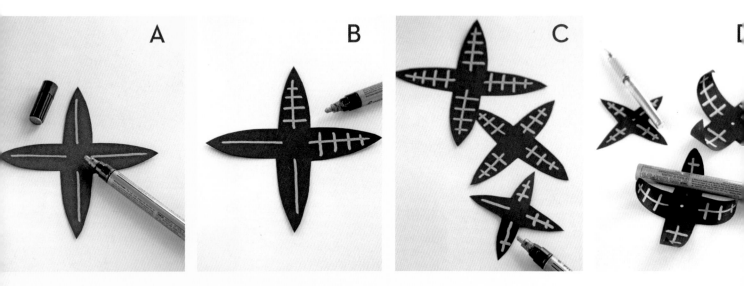

A   B   C   D

how to:

1 Print out the template on page 122. Use it to cut out the first set of flower petals with the craft knife. Each flower is made up of three sets of petals. After you have one complete set out of cardstock, trace around those on subsequent pieces of cardstock to make as many flowers as you want. Six makes a garland about 3 feet long.

2 Draw a center line on each segment of each petal as shown in photo A. Repeat this on all three petals. Draw shorter lines up and down the segments that cross the center line at a 90° angle (photo B).

3 Each petal set gets this crosshatching treatment, but the largest gets four crossing lines, the medium petal gets three crossing lines, and the smallest petals get two (photo C).

4 Use the hole punch to make a small hole in the center of each petal. Roll each petal segment around the barrel of a pen to curl it up at the ends slightly. On the smallest petals use a thinner pen, the largest ones a fatter pen (photo D).

5 Stack the three petals, largest on bottom, then medium, then small on top, and secure with the brad. Twist them so that each set is at a 45 ° angle to the one below it (photo E).

6 Attach a short loop of string, yarn, or cord to the back of the flower using an inch-long piece of tape, as shown in photo F. Tie each flower onto a longer string or cord for hanging.

E

F

Glow-in-the-Dark TREAT BUCKETS

MATERIALS

lacy cut paper (find it in the scrapbooking section of your local craft store)

temporary spray-on adhesive plain metal bucket

glow-in-the-dark spray paint

optional: black latex paint (spray or brushable) for striped bucket

optional: spray-on clear finish to protect the painted design

TOOLS

scissors

masking tape

Pillowcases are out of the question these days. And those plastic pumpkins are just so uninspired. Send your trick-or-treaters out into the night with a bucket that glimmers and glows by day as well as by night. These plain buckets from the hardware store get a quick shot of glow-in-the-dark paint through an improvised stencil so they pack an extra punch even in the dark. If you are not a fan of florals or a connoisseur of curlicues, the striped bucket is a nice graphic touch. Or you could stencil an initial on the bucket to make it personal.

A

B

C

D

E

how to:

1 Cut the lacy paper so that it fits on your bucket. You may need to cut multiple pieces to wrap completely around the entire bucket. You also may need to cut a section out where the handle meets the bucket so the paper stencil will lie flat. Spray the stencil with the adhesive, and stick it firmly to the bucket (photo A).

2 Lightly spray the bucket with multiple coats of glow-in-the-dark paint (photo B).

3 Carefully remove the stencil from the metal bucket to reveal the stenciled design. Let dry completely (photo C).

4 For maximum glowiness, paint the inside of the bucket as well. Use a piece of newspaper to wrap the outside of the bucket, and secure it with masking tape around the top edge to protect the design on the outside. Spray multiple coats of the glow-in-the-dark paint on the interior. For a more long-lasting bucket, spray the entire painted surface with clear finish (photo D).

ALTERNATE STRIPED BUCKET: I discovered this cool effect quite by accident, although faux painters know this technique well. I first sprayed this bucket with black high-gloss latex paint and let it dry. Then I taped off stripes about $1^1/_2$ inches wide with masking tape. Then I sprayed on the enamel-based glow-in-the-dark paint. Because the compositions of the two paint formulas are not wholly compatible, the glow-in-the-dark paint cracked and peeled over the black latex. But happily, it made a really cool distressed surface that was perfect for the general disaster and distress theme of the Halloween season (photo E).

The glow-in-the-dark paints that are available at your local hardware store do a nice job of recharging their glow under normal light. Depending on the manufacturer, it takes between 2 and 8 hours for the paint to have a full "charge." It should then glow for a couple of hours at least.

WALL HANGING

Who knew that owls, when handled just right, could look as menacing as skulls or like grimacing jack-o'-lanterns? Depending on your skill with a needle and thread, and how much time you're willing to commit, you can hand sew the owls in place, or just use a permanent spray-on adhesive to keep them from flying away. The cutting and piecing is kind of like a fun little puzzle. And the graphic black and white makes a strong statement that blurs the boundaries between craft and art.

MATERIALS

1 1/2 yards of black felt (you'll have leftovers)

1/2 yard of cream or white felt (use a wool or wool blend felt for a much nicer finished product)

temporary spray adhesive

orange embroidery floss

18-inch dowel

1 1/2 yards of ribbon for hanging

optional: permanent spray-on fabric adhesive

TOOLS

scissors

measuring tape or yard stick

embroidery or tapestry needle

straight pins

how to:

1 Measure and cut a piece of black felt 18 inches wide by 52 inches long.

2 Print out the owl templates on page 123. Spray the back of the paper templates with temporary adhesive, and stick down on the white or cream felt (photo A).

3 Using sharp scissors, cut around the owl design to cut away the black area of the design. Note that these pieces will NOT be one continuous piece. Many of the owl designs will have multiple pieces (photo B).

4 When you are trying to cut away an area that starts on the inside of the design, fold the paper and felt in half, and cut a small bite with your scissors. Then you can put your scissors in that slit to continue cutting out the design (photo C).

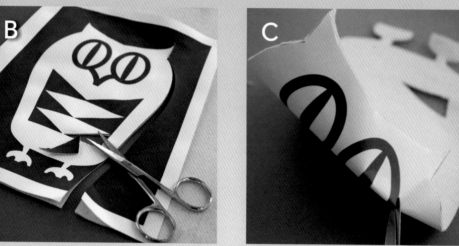

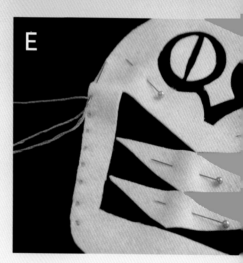

5 Remove the paper from the cut owl. The felt will still be tacky on this side, so place this side facedown so the residual glue keeps it in place while you are stitching it. Starting down about 6 to 8 inches from the top of the black banner, center the first owl design and pin in place (photo D).

6 If you choose to use the permanent adhesive instead of stitching to attach the owls, remove the paper, then spray the same side with permanent adhesive and position the owls as though you were stitching.

7 Stitch around the perimeter of the white owl pieces about $1/8$ inch in from the edge. You will have to go all the way around the large pieces, but some of the smaller pieces (like the eyes) can just be stitched once down the middle. A thimble might come in handy if you find it hard to get the needle through the fabric (photo E).

8 Each subsequent owl starts 4 to 6 inches below the one before it.

9 When all the owls are in place, fold down the top edge of the banner 2 to 4 inches (depending on the thickness of your dowel). Pin in place. Either hand or machine stitch this fold down to make the dowel pocket. Slide the dowel into the pocket. Cut the ribbon pieces to about 18 to 24 inches each, and tie them to each end of the dowel. Tie the other ends together in the middle to allow the banner to hang. If there is excess black felt at the bottom, just cut it off to suit your size.

Pumpkin Print
NAPKINS & TREAT BAGS

Halloween has always been a food holiday for kids, because—let's face facts—it is all about the treats. Grown-ups are just realizing that Halloween is a great excuse to sit down to some autumn deliciousness. But who can stomach those garish orange paper products that dot the tablescape this time of year? These hand-printed originals are much more of a feast for the eyes, and can be made in barely a blink.

MATERIALS

1 yard plain fabric (muslin, linen, hopsacking are all good)

one medium-sized potato

fabric paint or ink in black or dark gray

a couple small tidbits of cardstock to improvise stamped shapes

permanent fabric markers in green and orange

optional: sewing machine with black thread

TOOLS

scissors

cutting board

knife

paper plate for paint

73

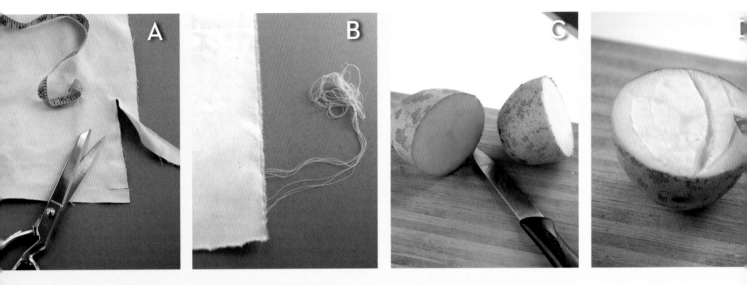

how to:

1 Measure out the fabric and mark the corners of a 33-inch square. With the tips of the scisssors, make a short snip at the corner. Then using this as a starting point, tear the fabric along that line. This creates a nice frayed edge for the napkins. Repeat with the snips and the tears until you have a 33-inch square with all the edges frayed. Now fold the square in half, and snip and tear the halfway point. Then fold each of these pieces in half, then snip and tear them in half. You now have four napkins, each about 16 inches square, with four frayed edges (photo A).

2 Augment the fraying along all the edges by tearing threads, one at a time, off the edges. Work your way around all the edges until you have about 1/4 inch of frayed edge on each napkin (photo B).

3 To make the print, cut your potato in half as shown. Use the tip of the knife to carve four curving lines into the surface as shown to make a simple abstract pumpkin. Be sure to clear out enough of the potato pulp so that the print lines will be distinct (photos C and D).

4 Make a few test prints to make sure you have the hang of it before printing your napkins. Position the fabric on a soft surface—a couple of layers of news-paper or cardstock will do. Fill up a small paper plate with fabric paint (photo E) or use an ink pad charged with fabric inks. Dip your potato facedown into the paint or ink, and then press it firmly on the napkin (photo F). The edges of the potato print should be 1/2 to 3/4 inch from the edge of the napkin to allow for a little extra fraying as well as some edge stitching, if you'd like.

E

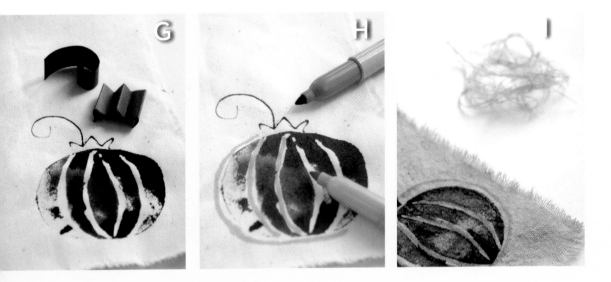

how to: (continued)

5 Make very simple stamps for the pumpkin details using small scraps of cardstock. Cut two pieces of cardstock about 2 inches wide by 1 inch tall. Fold one accordion style so it has three peaks and valleys. Roll the other into a tight spiral, then allow it to relax a bit to form a gentle curve (as shown in photo G). Dip the edge of these two pieces into your ink, and use the accordion fold to create abstract leaves on the pumpkin and the curved piece to create a stem.

6 With the orange fabric marker, outline the pumpkin and the vertical lines in orange. Add a curve and a squiggle of green to finish off the stem and leaves (photo H).

7 Pull away additional threads from the edges to increase the amount of fray if you would like (photo I).

8 The napkins can be called "done" now if you want to keep it casual. Or you can add a line of black machine stitching around the perimeter about 1/2 inch in from the edge to make the napkins complete.

Make simple treat bags or party favors with this same technique. This time, tear pieces that are about 5 inches wide by 8 to 10 inches tall. Print with the potato as before and add the embellishments as you see fit. Machine stitch down the sides and across the bottom to make a small bag, then fill it with treats and tie it closed with a ribbon.

Crazy-Stitched & Patched
APRONS

black cotton chef's apron with bib
(available at craft stores and
restaurant supply)

calico fabric scraps in shades of
orange and green

white thread

felt scraps in cream, orange,
and gold

TOOLS

scissors

sewing machine

straight pins

white pencil

needle

Whether your Halloween menu includes deviled eggs, rib-eye roast, or Bloody Marys, things can get messy in the kitchen this time of year. These customized chef's aprons will take the hit so you don't have to. A bit of wild stitching and a hint of color make these plain black aprons come to life. The effect is chaotic but contained, chic but not meek. This is a quick and easy way to sew something even if you are more hipster than seamster. Let someone else do the boring stuff, and pick up the plain, black chef's aprons at a craft store or restaurant supply spot. Then fire up your sewing machine and let 'er rip.

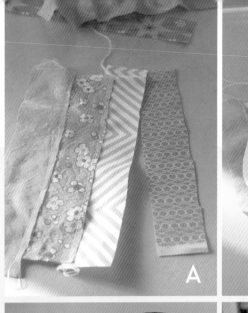

A

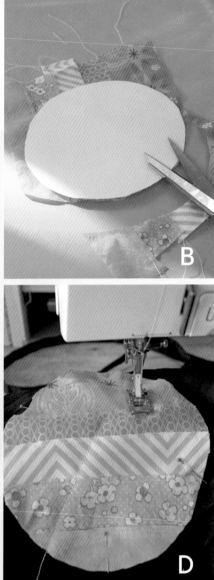

B

C

D

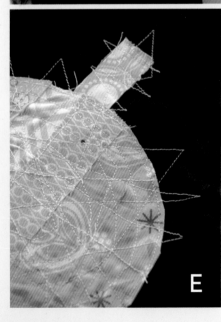

E

how to:

FOR THE PATCHWORK PUMPKIN APRON:

1 Cut 6 pieces of printed cotton in or-ange-y tones. Each piece should measure about 2 inches by 8 inches. Sew the first two pieces together overlapping the raw edges about ¼ inch. Continue overlapping and sewing the strips together until all are used (photo A).

2 Cut an oval from a piece of paper that is about 6 by 8 inches. Use this piece as a template to cut an oval out of your patch-work fabric (photo B).

3 Cut a piece of green-toned calico cotton ¾ inch by 3 inches for the stem. Center the pieced oval on the apron bib, and tuck the green stem under the top edge. Secure everything in place with a few straight pins (photo C).

4 Begin sewing across the face of the pumpkin, starting a little off the edge and continuing on beyond the opposite edge. To turn, leave the needle down in the fab-ric, but pick up the pressure foot, spin the fabric and the apron around, and start sewing in another direction. Make some of the turns very sharp angles and some less so. Be sure to go beyond the edge of the pumpkin on most passes, but vary the amount you go into the black (photo D).

5 Do shorter, tighter passes of stitching across the stem to sew it into place. Do one line of stitching straight up with a steep angle at the top to add some visual energy to the stem.

6 Finish the pumpkin by sewing around the perimeter. If you'd like, spiral that pe-rimeter stitching inward and keep making tighter and tighter concentric circles un-til you get to the middle of the pumpkin (photo E).

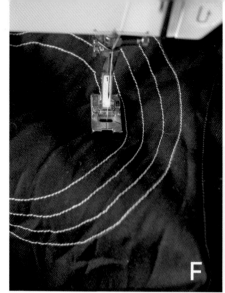

Additionally...

You can add more chaos to this apron by making some sharp, angular stitching across the hem. Think erratic heartbeat as you are sewing. Add a second row of stitched peaks and valleys for interest (photo J).

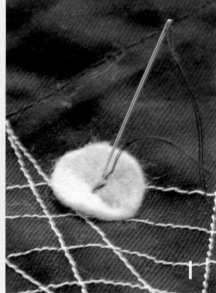

how to:

FOR THE ABSTRACT PUMPKIN APRON:

1 Cut out a circle about 7 inches in circumference (a salad plate works well). Trace around this to draw a circular shape on the apron bib. Then, starting at the outside edge, begin sewing around the perimeter. At the top, angle in so that the next circle is about 1/4 to 3/8 inch from the first revolution. Continue spiraling in, spinning the apron around as you go, until you have stitched to the center of the circle (photo F).

2 Now begin sewing across the circle in straight lines. Sew out beyond the edge of the spiral circle, pivot on your needle, and sew at a different angle across the circle in another direction. Repeat many times (photo G).

3 To create a little extra graphic and textural interest, occasionally stop in the middle of a straight line of stitching, and run the stitching back and forth at slightly different angles, to make a little "node." You can also pick up the presser foot and move it a 1/4 inch to leave a little loose thread. Then stitch over it on the next pass. These are supposed to look a little chaotic and messy (photo H).

4 For your last straight pass, sew straight out from the top of the circle a few inches to create a "stem." Then do lots of short, sharp-angled stitching passes across the straight up line to further create the look of a stem.

5 Hand sew on little circles of colored felt or of calico prints to add color to the mix. Random placement and contrasting colored thread make this a nice touch (photo I).

A PECK *of* PRETTY PECULIAR PUMPKINS

Full disclosure: I hate carving pumpkins. I know, this is scandalous news coming from someone writing a Halloween book. But what is fun about jabbing a razor sharp knife, glistening with slippery pumpkin juice, into the slimy flesh of a ridiculously thick-skinned gourd. Seems ill-suited to tactile enjoyment and creative abandon. And don't even get me started on the weird raw pumpkin smell... Anyway, suffice it to say, here are a dozen ways to make beautifully beguiling pumpkins armed only with pens and paints, and nothing sharper than a thumbtack. Added bonus: All these pumpkins will last for weeks, as opposed to carved pumpkins that can hardly survive one night.

ILLUSTRATED PUMPKINS

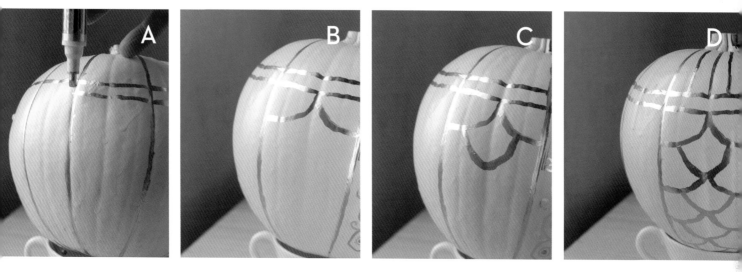

A B C D

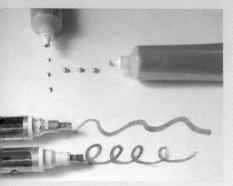

MATERIALS

small to medium orange
or white pumpkins

gold and silver leafing pens

gold and silver metallic
puffy paint

optional: white or cream
spray paint

a teacup or small bowl to
hold the pumpkin while
you work

how to:

1 If you are using orange
pumpkins, spray paint them
white and let dry completely.

2 With the gold pen, start at
the top of the pumpkin near
the stem and draw vertical
lines down in every other of
the natural "valleys" of the
pumpkin. Then draw two horizontal lines around the top
third of the pumpkin (photo A).

3 Add two quarter circles as
shown in photo B.

4 Then add a semi-circle below that, as in photo C.

5 Repeat this fish-scale pattern within this vertical section down to the bottom of
the pumpkin. Add three

evenly spaced vertical lines in
the top section above those
horizontal lines, as shown in
photo D.

6 Rotate the pumpkin clockwise, skip one of the vertical
sections that you drew in
step 2, and then repeat this
fish-scale pattern in the next
vertical section.

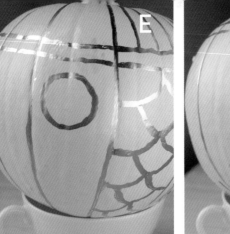

7 In the next blank vertical section over, start by drawing a circle toward the top. Make the circle small enough so the edge of the circle is almost 1/2 inch away from the vertical line on either side (photo E).

8 Draw the next circle down so its top edge just touches the circle above it, and it too clears the vertical lines on either side by about 1/2 inch. Continue drawing smaller and smaller circles until you are at the bottom of the pumpkin (photo F).

9 In the space above the horizontal lines, draw one vertical line to divide the space in half, then draw three increasingly small circles (photo G).

10 Add another smaller concentric circle within each of the circles drawn in step 8. Switch to a silver leafing pen, and add simple curlicues at the top edge of each of the circles, as shown in photo H.

11 Finally, use the silver puffy paint to add dots throughout the design (photo I). Check out the pumpkin on page 86 to see where all the dots should go.

$\mathcal{O}r\ldots$

Here is a quick visual breakdown of yet another variation on the drawn pumpkin. Taking it step-by-step, line-by-line uncomplicates the process. As you can see, though the finished product looks intricate, the process is really quite simple, and requires only the most rudimentary drawing skill and only a moderately steady hand. Turn to page 122 for an illustration that shows yet one more drawn pumpkin variation.

Swagged Pumpkin

A

B

C

D

E

F

G

MATERIALS

small to medium orange pumpkin

metallic silver spray paint

T-headed pins, white and gold pearl-headed pins

silver and gold chain from the jewelry-making department of your local craft store

assorted silver beads in a variety of sizes

small, narrow, flat-head nail about 2 to 3 inches long or, use a head pin (find them in the jewelry department of your craft store)

TOOLS

wire cutters

small hammer

how to:

1 Spray-paint your pumpkin with the silver/chrome paint. You may need a couple coats. Let dry completely.

2 Use a T-headed pin to attach the end of the chain to the pumpkin near the base of the stem (photo A).

3 Stretch the chain down to the bottom of the pumpkin (staying in one of the vertical "valleys." Pin the chain at the base (photo B).

4 Bring the chain up again in the "valley" that is a couple over, stretch it taut, then pin it at the base of the stem (photo C). Angle the chain toward another valley, and send it down that one. Pin to anchor as before. Repeat until you have worked all the way around the pumpkin. Cut the chain with wire cutters.

5 Anchor each chain at the midway point using a gold pearl-headed pin and a bead (photo D).

6 To add the swags, anchor the ends of both the gold and the silver chain with a bead and a white pearl-headed pin in the space between the vertical chains. These new anchor pins should sit higher on the pumpkin than the earlier ones. Drape the two chains down and under the earlier anchor pins, letting the gold chain drape lower than the silver. Pin the two chains in place as shown in photo E. Continue working your way all around the pumpkin. To finish, measure the final swag, then cut the two chains with wire cutters. Use the same anchor pin that secured the beginning of the chains to anchor their ends.

7 To add the fancy finial on the top, stack a series of interesting beads, large and small, on the nail. Sink the nail into the stem of the pumpkin right up to the bottommost bead. A tap or two with a small hammer might help things along (photos F and G).

STUDDED PUMPKINS

MATERIALS

small to medium orange
pumpkin

gold metalic spray paint

decorative thumb tacks,
nailheads, upholstery tacks,
etc.

beads for top finial
long pin or long narrow nail
for top finial

how to:

1 This really couldn't be simpler. Start by choosing a fun array of beautiful up-holstery tacks and decorative nail heads. Check at your favorite hardware store, but there are also lots of sources online where the possibilities are dizzying.

2 Paint your pumpkins with gold or silver metalic paint. Let dry completely. Or you can leave the pumpkin in its natural orange. That looks good with tacks added, too.

3 Begin adding tacks in the pattern of your choosing. Press them firmly into the pumpkin flesh. A little pumpkin juice might ooze out, but just wipe it away.

4 Finish your five-minute masterpiece with a finial using the technique de-scribed on page 91.

Thread-Wrapped Pumpkins

MATERIALS

small to medium orange pumpkin

black and white spray paint

decorative thumbtacks

white and black embroidery floss

TOOLS

scisssors

how to:

1 Spray-paint your pumpkins and let them dry thoroughly.

2 Start with a row of thumbtacks running horizontally around the middle of the pumpkin. Space the tacks so they are in every OTHER valley as you go around the pumpkin.

3 Add another row of thumbtacks higher up near the stem. These should be placed in the center between the tacks you put in around the middle of the pumpkin. Add another row just like this one down on the bottom of the pumpkin near the base (photo A).

4 Starting on the bottom row, wrap the embroidery floss around the first thumbtack, then send the floss up and over the thumbtack on the row above. Next it should go down and under the next tack on the bottom row (photo B).

5 Continue stretching the thread up and down, over and under the tacks on the two bottom rows until you have worked all the way around the pumpkin (photo C). Go around the same path one more time to double the floss.

(continued on page 97)

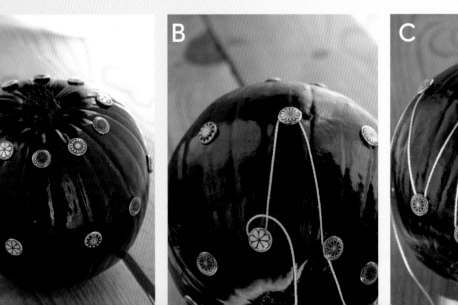

A

B

C

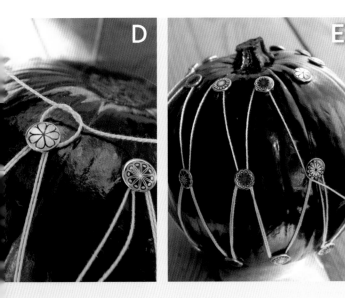

how to: (continued)

6 Tie off the thread on the bottom row (photo D).

7 Repeat steps 4 and 5 again, this time alternating the embroidery floss between the middle and the top row of thumbtacks. Add a second round of floss to double it as before (photo E).

8 Without tying off the thread, start working horizontally on the top row of thumbtacks. Send the thread up and over the first tack, and wrap it all the way around in a clockwise direction. Now take the thread down and under the next tack, again wrapping it all the way around, but this time in a counterclockwise direction. Repeat on all the tacks in this top row. Don't double the thread this time, and don't tie off (photo F).

9 Lastly, put a tack in the middle of the pumpkin stem, and now wrap the thread from the top row of tacks to the tack on the stem. Then come back to the same top row tack. Now move over one, doubling the horizontal thread, and wrap up and over the stem tack and back down again. Repeat, going all the way around the top row. Finish by tying off the thread (photo G).

SIMPLE PAINTED GOURDS

how to:

1 Starting near the stem, spiral the masking tape down the gourd leaving a uniform space about 1 inch wide between each circle of tape. You'll need to angle and fold the tape slightly so that it can circle smoothly around the gourd (as seen in the photo at left). Spiral all the way down to the bottom of the gourd.

2 Starting on the second row down from the top, cut away a section of the horizontal tape you just applied to make a 2-to 3-inch gap (photo A). Run a short section of tape vertically through this gap from the row above to the row below (see photos B & C).

3 Repeat step two around the entire gourd, spacing and alternating the vertical pieces. Once all the tape is in place, work around the entire surface, rubbing and pressing the tape down, and getting rid of puckers and air pockets (photo D).

4 Paint with craft paint using a small foam brush. Let the paint get mostly dry before removing tape. Use a damp cotton swab to clean up any unwanted paint blobs that snuck under the tape.

MATERIALS

$1/2$ or $3/4$-inch-wide masking tape

medium to large gourds

white or cream craft paint

TOOLS

scissors

small foam paintbrush

And...

Check out page 122 for a template that shows an alternate painting pattern.

STICKERED PUMPKINS

MATERIALS

orange or white pumpkins

self-adhesive dimensional stickers
(in the scrapbooking section at craft stores)

sequin pins (available at craft stores)

TOOLS

thimble

how to: Position the adhesive stickers in interesting patterns on
the surface of the pumpkin. Press firmly in place. Then secure the stickers
with the short sequin pins. Some thinner, smaller stickers are flexible enough
to stick completely with just the adhesive and won't require many pins.

FLOWERY PUMPKINS

MATERIALS

pumpkins (either real or fake) in orange or white

narrow ribbon in Halloween colors and interesting patterns

glue dots for the fake pumpkins or sequin pins for the real ones

TOOLS

scissors

MATERIALS

orange or white pumpkins

pearl-headed or straight pins

decorative paper flowers (at craft stores)

how to : Use the pins to attach the paper flowers around the mid-section of the pumpkin. You could carefully place them in a pattern with organized colors and sizes of flowers, or you can just scatter them about, in a spray of blooms, as shown here.

BERIBBONED PUMPKINS

how to:

For the white faux pumpkin: Starting at the stem, use glue dots to apply a strip of ribbon in the vertical valleys on a faux pumpkin. Cut the ribbon strips long enough so that it wraps all the way under the bottom of the pumpkin and ends on the other side of the stem. Repeat until all the valleys are beribboned.

For the real pumpkins: Use short pins (called "sequin pins") to secure the strips of ribbon in the vertical valleys of the pumpkin as descibed above. Add a contrasting ribbon around the "equator" of the pumpkin. Alternatively, tie a simple bow in a short piece of ribbon and pin it to the top of the pumpkin stem.

Quick-As-A-Wink
CUT FELT BEARDS

It doesn't take much to disguise a face. These goofy beards and mustaches make use of the simple technique we all used to make paper snowflakes as children to cut out felt facial hair that gives even the youngest reveler a bit of Halloween gravitas. The cuts in the fabric are graphic and strong, not unlike Maori tattoos. This elevates a simple concept that could easily have looked unsophisticated into a bit of artful fashion. Use good quality felt here to make the beards comfortable, preferably a rayon-wool blend.

A

B

C

D

E

MATERIALS

black or white felt

black or white elastic in a narrow
band ($1/8$ inch or $1/4$ inch work well)

TOOLS

sharp scissors

needle and thread

how to:

EACH BEARD OR MUSTACHE IS CUT FREE-FORM, AND WILL
BE AS UNIQUE AND SINGULAR AS A SNOWFLAKE:

For the white mustache

1 Cut a piece of felt 4 x 8 inches. Fold it in half the long
way. Use the template on page 126 to get a rough idea of
the shape to cut and where to put the mouth hole.   Cut out
the curlicue and the small linear clips that make the beard's
bottom edge.

2 Using a needle and thread, sew a piece of elastic about 8
to 10 inches long on the mask to hold it in place. Don't attach
the elastic to the very edge of the mustache, but in about
$1^{1}/_{2}$ inches from the edge as shown on the template. This will
make it fit better on your face (photo E).

For the short beard

1 Cut a piece of felt 5 x 8 inches. Fold it in half the long way.
Use the template on page 126
to get a rough idea of the shape
to cut and where to put the
mouth hole.   Follow the template for the cuts, or use your
imagination (photos A and B).

2 Repeat step 2 above.

For the long beard

1 Start with a piece of felt about 8 inches square, then follow steps 1 and 2 from above, but use the long beard template on page 126 (photos C and D).

Black Doily SPIDER WEBS

Add some drama to a simple tablescape or an unadorned window with these sprayed black doily spider webs. The intricate shapes and textures of these old doilies really are astoundingly beautiful. But most of us don't have the fussy Victorian homes that beg for them. So they languish, haunting junk stores and garage sales, where we see them in forlorn bundles wishing for a home. Well, let's give them one. Spray-paint them black and allow the doily webs to mimic the busy to-doings of the blackest of widows. It's scary how easy this is.

MATERIALS

crocheted doilies

black spray paint

black yarn or string

straight pins

tacks

TOOLS

scissors

needle and thread

how to:

FOR THE DOILY TABLE MATS:

Lay the doilies flat and spray paint with black paint. You will have to make several passes with the paint to saturate the material with color. Let dry, then flip over, and spray paint the other side until all the light-colored areas are covered, and the doily is a rich black. Hang to dry.

FOR THE WINDOW TREATMENT:

The spray painted doilies can either be attached to existing sheer curtains, or you can temporarily hang simple white muslin fabric in your windows as a backdrop.

1 Pin the doilies onto the curtain or cloth. Thread a needle with black thread, tack the doily onto the curtuan with a few little stitches in two or three places around the perimeter. Repeat with as many doily "webs" as you'd like.

2 Tie the black yarn to the edge of the doily and crisscross the surface of the curtain. Attach the yarn to tacks in the window frames to stretch taut. Be sure that the yarn makes its way to all the webs on the curtain's surface just as spider's silk would.

MATERIALS

large poster board in
multiple colors

staples

masking tape or small round stickers

TOOLS

tailors' measuring tape (or use a
piece of string and ruler)

craft scissors

stapler

Instant Halloween
PAPER HATS

What to do if Halloween sneaks up on you and you need a fun costume fast? Make these quick, five-minute hats using just your scissors and a stapler. They come together easily, are whimsical and fun, and cost almost nothing. A stapler is the ultimate tool to put these no-pattern hats together, though you'll need to cover the staples on the inside with small stickers or masking tape to safeguard delicate skin. Whether you are outfitting a princess, making a viking, crowning a king, or invoking the court jester, these hats are meant to be experimental and playful and shouldn't follow the instructions too closely. These play to the fun, frolicsome dressup side of Halloween rather than the spooky, creepy, scary side. They're not meant to be scary, just scary beautiful.

For Hat #1 Make a wavy hatband. Cut strips of paper 1 inch wide by 15 inches. Roll these strips into tight spirals. Make as many of these curlicues as you have peaks on your hatband. Attach each one with a staple. Make another band 1 inch wide by about 28 inches long so it fits around the hatband with some left over. Staple together as shown. Cut a small circle of paper, then staple the strip and the circle to the bottom edge of the hatband. Make incisions in the end of this "ribbon of paper," and curl those by hand to make a little hat ornament.

Hat **1**

For Hat #2 Cut four strips of paper 2 inches wide by about 30 inches long. Staple the ends to the top of the hatband in each of the cardinal directions. Make a slit in two of the bands with your scissors. Cut another contrasting color of paper 2 inches by about 12 to 18 inches. Feed that through the bands as shown. Cut two smaller pieces of that same paper about 6 inches long for use as "horns." Staple them at an angle to the crosspiece, on either end, then trim off the irregular angles and you're done.

For Hat #3 Cut a large arc of paper about 12 inches long and 8 inches high. Cut some large triangular bites out of the top edge to make a shape reminiscent of a dinosaur. Cut a slit fore and aft on the hatband, and slide the scaly top piece in place as shown. Cut a small, brightly colored strip of paper about 1 inch x 8 inches long. Attach two contrasting circles of paper to each end to be the "eyes." Cut a slit in the top piece toward the front as shown and a smaller slit in the center of the eye strip, and seat it in the slit.

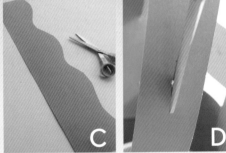

Notes: A Each hat begins with a 3-to 4-inch-wide hatband. You can use a tape measure or string to measure the wearer's head, or you can just wrap the paper around their head and mark the size, leaving about 3 inches of overlap. **B** Staple in two places as shown. **C** You can cut the hatband wavy or pointy for a unique design. **D** Some designs require a slit cut in one of the hat pieces. Use a hole punch to start the slit if desired, then cut the rest with scissors. **E** Staples can be sharp and scratchy, so cover all the exposed staples on the inside of the hat with small round stickers or with masking tape.

For Hat #4 Follow the instructions for hat #2, but use twice as many strips going up and over, and alternate the colors. Press down in the center of the hat, and crease the strips so they now have a regal angle to them as shown. Add a triangular topknot if you'd like.

Hat **3**

Hat **4**

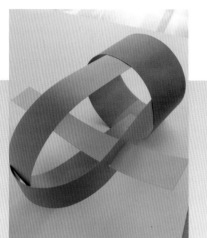
Hat **2**

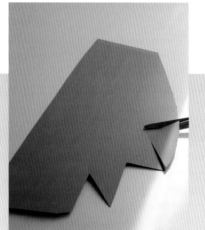

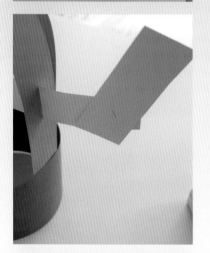

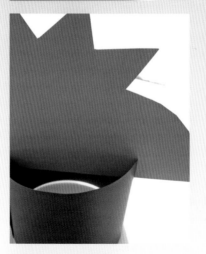

YARD SPECTER

Inviting a ghoul into your yard for a visit is not recommended at any other time of year than on Halloween. Luckily, this one takes only minutes to set up, but has all the spooky animation and looming presence that you could ever want. Use metal fence posts from the hardware store as the base, then wrap them with white holiday lights, and swathe it all in layers of sheer fabric. The combination of fluttering fabric and glowing, glittering light makes this simple sculpture the quintessential shape shifter; the tiniest breath of wind brings it to life.

MATERIALS

one stake (perforated metal fence post works great) about 5 feet tall

one crosspiece of same about 3 feet long

wing nut and bolt to attach crosspiece to stake

one string of white LED holiday lights (15 to 20 feet long is plenty)

2 to 3 yards each sheer fabric like gauze, netting, sheer taffeta, or metallic sheer. (I used a gray and a black sheer, and a silver metallic sheer.)

duct tape or twist ties

large safety pins

TOOLS

sledgehammer, or post-hammering tool for getting the stake in the ground

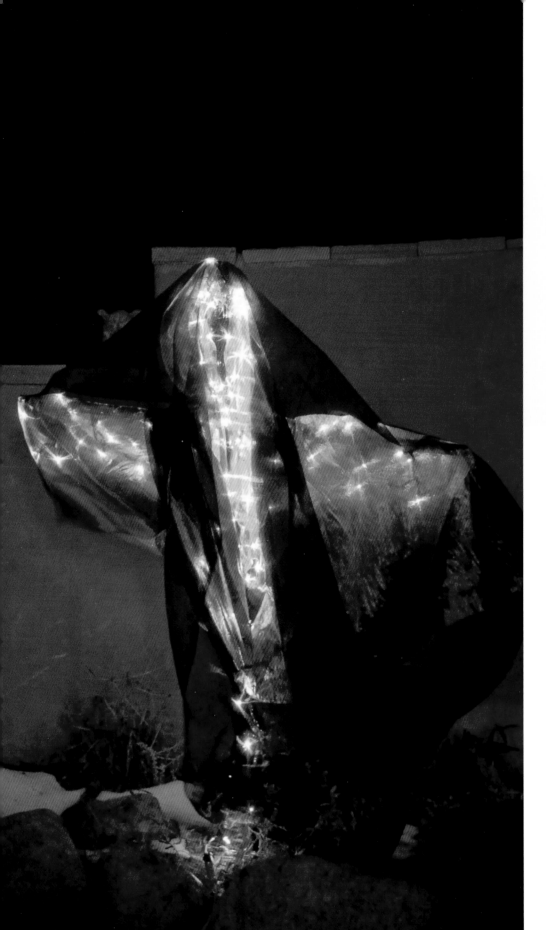

how to:

1 Using the holes already in the stake, center the crosspiece side to side and about 12 to 15 inches down from the top of the stake. Match up the nearest holes (photo A).

2 Use the wing nut and the bolt to secure the two metal bars together at right angles. A washer might help if you can't get it to tighten down enough to prevent slipping. Plant the stake in the ground (photo B).

3 Plug in your lights and, starting at the bottom, wrap them up the center post. Be generous with the lights, and wrap loosely. Use the little notched clips in the posts to hold the lights or, alternatively, use small strips of duct tape. Wrap the lights up the center stake, then out to the end of each arm and back again, then up to the top of the ghoul's "head" (photo C).

4 Wrap the first sheer piece of fabric around the stakes and crossbar as shown. Use the safety pins through the holes in the metal bars to secure the fabric. Next, use the metallic sheer to wrap. Finish with the black sheer and be sure to wrap this piece all the way down to the base of the stake and secure it with duct tape (photos D – F).

MATERIALS

recycled cans: 2 soup cans, 3 small coffee cans, and 1-gallon paint can with lid

large metal washers

baling wire

one metal funnel at least 5 inches in diameter

TOOLS

drill with bit suitable for drilling a 3/16 inch hole in metal

Tin Can

TIN MAN

Here's a scarecrow that would never be frightened of a match. Made from recycled tin cans and a few nuts and bolts, this guy will keep watch over your door or porch and keep all but the scariest ghouls at bay. You could find rusty cans, or even paint some for this project. However, the shiny cans, lifted from the recycle bin, give him a certain jaunty attitude that makes him all the more endearing.

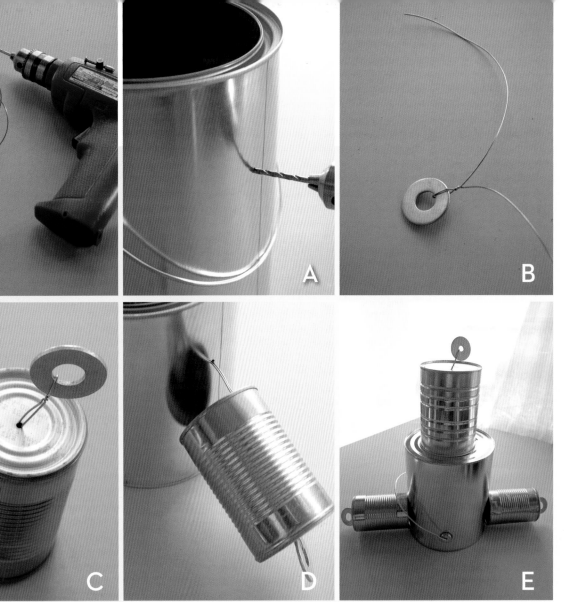

how to:

1 Drill a hole about 3 inches down on each side of the large paint can where the arms will go (photo A). Drill a hole centered in the bottom of each soup can.

2 Cut a piece of wire about 4 feet long. Thread it through the hole in the washer, and fold the wire in half over the washer. Twist the two pieces of wire around each other a few times to secure the washer (photo B).

3 Thread the two ends of wire through the hole in the "arm" can (photo C).

4 Thread the two ends of the wire in through the hole in one side of the paint can and then out through the other hole (photo D). Thread the other soup can "arm" over the two pieces of wire and out through the hole. Attach another metal washer to the two wire ends, and twist the wire until the can arms are held tautly in place (photo E).

5 For legs, start by drilling two holes in the bottom of the paint can about 4 to 6 inches apart. Then drill holes in the bottom of the two coffee can "legs." Follow a similar procedure to step 4 to attach the legs, this time threading the wire up through one hole in the paint can bottom, then down through the other.

G

6 For the head, drill a hole in the center of the paint can lid. Cut a 2-foot length of wire. Wrap one end of the wire multiple times around a small bolt, then thread the end of the wire through the hole in the lid (photo F).

7 Send the wire up through the small coffee can "head," then through the spout of the inverted funnel "hat." Attach another metal washer to the wire at the top of the spout, and tighten down (photo G).

8 Reposition the lid on the paint can base, and gently but firmly hammer into place. Your tin man is ready to hang (photo H).

H

TEMPLATES & ILLUSTRATIONS
...and other important things

SIMPLE PAINTED GOURD --- Page 98

ILLUSTRATED PUMPKIN #3 --- Page 86

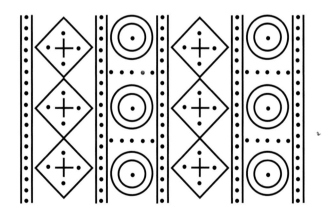

BLACK SKELETON FLOWER GARLAND --- Page 60

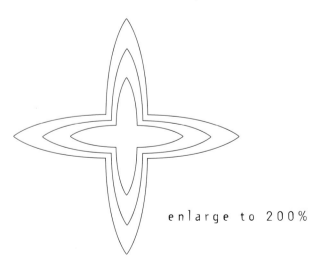

enlarge to 200%

enlarge to 200%

SPOOKY SPIRITS BOTTLE WRAPS --- Page 52

GONE BATTY NOTE CARDS --- Page 40

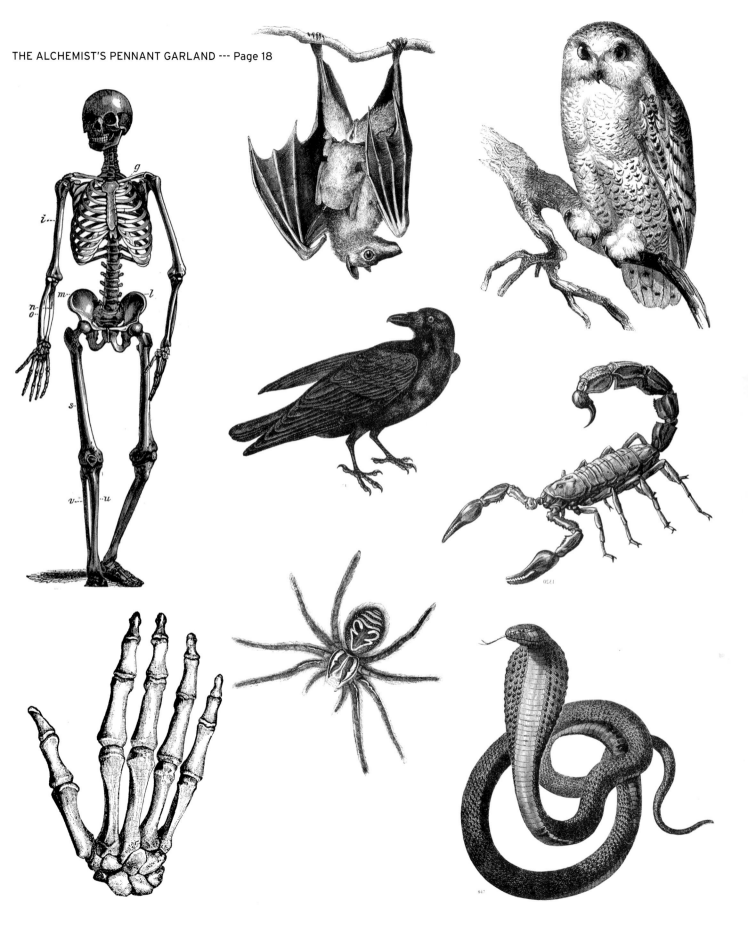

TEMPLATES & ILLUSTRATIONS
...and other important things

LONG BEARD-- Page 104

Fold Line—in half

Fold Line—in quarters

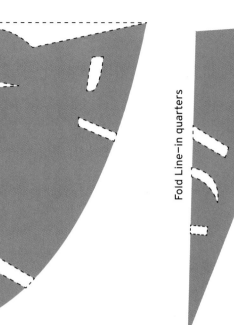

enlarge to 150%

SHORT BEARD-- Page 105

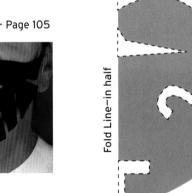

Fold Line—in half

MUSTACHE-- Page 104

Fold Line—in half

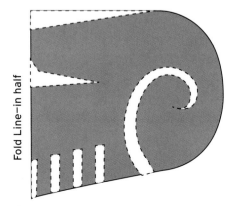

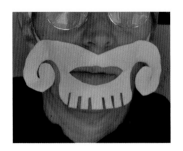

Acknowledgments:

Thanks to Karen Van Dusen for her tireless enthusiasm and her most fabulous all-hands-on-deck, pitch-in-anytime, no-idea-is-too-crazy spirit. She is my go-to location scout, talent coordinator, prop finder and all around co-conspirator. Thanks as well to Nicole McConville for coming up with the idea and insisting I do the book. To Linda Kopp who has now heard every conceivable excuse for lateness, large and small, in every guise, scary and otherwise. Your simple trust, your calm encouragement, your gentle steering, and your most excellent ideas and advice have gotten me through. To my kids for teaching me that Halloween is about fun and frivolity and silly theater, and that it is worth every effort at being creative and unique.